W9-CLN-889

F O R T H   A   R A V E N

FORTH A RAVEN

POEMS BY Christina Davis

Alice James Books

FARMINGTON, MAINE

10 9 8 7 6 5 4 3 2 1

Alice James Books are published by Alice James Poetry Cooperative, Inc., an affiliate of the University of Maine at Farmington.

ALICE JAMES BOOKS

238 MAIN STREET

FARMINGTON, ME 04938

www.alicejamesbooks.org

Library of Congress Cataloging-in-Publication Data

Davis, Christina, 1971–

Forth a raven / Christina Davis.

   p. cm.

ISBN-13: 978–1–882295–57–9 (pbk.)

ISBN-10: 1–882295–57–9 (pbk.)

1. Title.

PS3604.A9562F67 2006

811'.6—dc22   2006004529

Alice James Book gratefully acknowledges support from the University of Maine at Farmington and the National Endowment for the Arts. 🌱

Cover photograph by Deborah Luster

CONTENTS

ACKNOWLEDGMENTS

Grateful acknowledgment is made to the following publications in which these poems first appeared: *Colorado Review:* "In the Shrine of the Holy Dirt"; *Jubilat:* "Homesickness" and "Birds of Every Wing Shall Dwell Within" (as "Worry-Worn God"); *LIT Magazine:* "Forth A Raven," "Advertisement for the Mountain" and "The Sadness of the Lingua Franca"; and *Pequod:* "O Who May Abide".

This book was written in honor of my friends and family whose love and wisdom have guided and sustained me on my journey: Nancy Wheeler, Jaclyn Friedman, Andrew Howell, Zack and Marla Vogel, Tona Barkley, Leigh Hays, David Rodin, Andrew Ginzel, Sarah Walker, Chris Edgar, and my beloved brother Rob and his family. And to my parents, John and Beverly Davis, who are the loves of my life, and to their parents and to the steamboat captains and architects and singers who sent me forth, my speechless thanks.

I am profoundly grateful to the MacDowell Colony and to Yaddo for their generous support, and to my mentors and advocates both early and late (Mary Jo Bang, Kathleen Ossip, Yerra Sugarman, Miranda Field, Susan Bruce, Rynn Williams), and to Catherine Barnett for her inimitable editorial eye and her unshakable faith.

FOR MY PARENTS

I

In the dream, we take god out of the attic and put back the birds,

higher than human
but horizontal, the whole of their bodies

is ahead, hazarded
like a question. Every question

      I have ever asked could be ground down to

Do you love me? Will I die?

      To which the birds reply,

            We came in full view

            of an island
            or a continent, for we knew

            not whether.

ADVERTISEMENT FOR THE MOUNTAIN

There are two versions of every life.

In the first one, you get a mother, a father,
your very own room,
a dandelion's-worth of chances.

You learn to walk, which is only done by walking.
You learn the past tense of *have*, which is *hunger*.

You learn to ask almost anything
is to ask it to be over,
as when the lover asks the other

"Are you sleeping? Are you beginning
to go away?"

(And whether or not you learn it, life does not penetrate
more than five miles above the earth
or reach more than three miles beneath the sea.

Life is eight miles long.

You could walk it, and be there before sundown.
Or swim it, or fall it, or crawl it.)

The second is told from the point
of view of the sky.

O WHO MAY ABIDE

From what have you fallen, what might you best have been?

Were you taught by strangers
to become a stranger, even as a child?

What can you not be told apart from, what is it you match,
as the creatures match
the mud, the snow, the sky, the grass?

Why do you say *dear god*,
as if you were writing to him?

If you strayed far, would the dog recognize you,
would your name no longer be famous
as it was in the mother's mouth? Is this what you mean

by *human* that you keep on
being born, till there is no house

for where you are headed?

THE OUTSET

I

It is 7:30. It is still possible
to know where you are.

The field quiet and birded, across it a deer has fled
and then turned back
as if it left some part of itself behind,
the part that feared me.

II

Which is harder, do you think, the journey to paradise
or the one to the underworld,
if on either occasion you know from the outset

you will have to return?

III

Before there was a self, there were many hunches,

many came to the cradle
but in going began
to define me as what-does-not-go-away.

IV

We are each what never leaves us, what we never see
the back of
is the self. But what loves us

is at the back, as Eurydice was
escorting him out
without his knowing.

V

It is eight o'clock, it is ten. It is time.

Home begins
in the mind, a dream

of walking.

Each time we moved,

I wanted to come back as a tree
and each time we stayed, as a bird.

Does anyone ever ask to return as himself again?

I wanted to be a tree
and myself-seeing-the-tree,

a bird and myself-being-the-bird.

O creatures-in-law…

THE HALF-LIFE

During the picnic,

he broke it to me about his having someone else back home.
Within a sentence, she was a wife.

I thanked him for telling me
as one thanks a waiter
for removing the meal.

Then he buried his head in my knees.

The body wears these moments on the outside, like a rose
we say is red, when red is only a moment
in the rose's motion from green to brown and when it is dead
the earth is a rose on the inside. If I listened closely,

I could hear the conjunction
forming before my name was "or."

I think he could hear it also,
something hinging
and coming un. But not to whom

or what we were
the alternative.

IN SEARCH OF A JURY

Have I never been mistaken
by the fox for the rabbit?

A man has been as jailed as he was innocent,
a girl as killed as she was young.

Am I not still and hare-like?
Don't I give off the least reek of meat?

There is a creaking commotion in the greens.
There have been foxes at the berries,

like calves at the teat. Am I not many and sweet
as the bushes, doesn't the gnat enjoy me

in plenty of places?
I know what the blue jays are after.

There is no learning to love
without incident.

MONADNOCK

We turned around at the mountain but not without ending
the loneliness of the ranger. *The mountain closes*
at dusk, he said, *though if you're already on it, you can still come down.*

I got older in your company,
but the day got older faster like a dog.

Though we had no dog, just something urgent and uncurbed
to which the climbers knelt,
calling *Come* and *Here* to, as who would not

if given the chance?

URBAN HYMN

I do not know an apple's worth.
It must be a little
less than a rose is, more than a tulip.
And cheaper than the lily
is the grass. I cannot tell a raven from a crow
or point to the front of the sun,
though I've looked
rain in the face, why some things are
only as they are falling.

Today, a woman stopped and asked
which way was west.
West what? I said, expecting a number,
a street. Whoever invented streets
must be rich by now.

Or sued, for how many are lost—
minus stars, minus meander.

WAVE HILL

The purple water lily closed.

I could not tell what it was closing, though—
a door, a mouth.

A bee got out in the nick of time.

I thought if we can't come to any conclusion,
let the flower.

Then I saw how the lily in its closure remained
aimed, like palms
in prayer to no god in particular.

Above us, birds traveled together and gunward.

If they must fall, I thought,
let the falling be faster. We practice

on earth, which loves not the amateur.

Let *amateur* mean
what is done out of love.

BORDER PATROL

This is how the spider feels
an inch from the web.

To know is to know the difference.

When you ask your lover what he is thinking,
aren't you really asking

Do I occur to you? do I take place?

Sometimes to walk toward anyone
is the wilderness.

You followed a boy once
along the White Cliffs. When a rock

slipped, he said,
France got larger.

II

THE SADNESS OF THE LINGUA FRANCA

In Bird, I speak brokenly. Hiss and flail and never learn.

And the swan will never mouth
the noun for *bread*,
the declensions of *crumb*. Though I could stop

its migration with a crumb.

After English, we never do get to be strangers again.

The language is famous and followed,
it has no loneliness left.

It has made it to the moon. It has got god
to speak it. It will get
to everything first, if it can.

But not the swan, pale as a page
I will never have written.

ANY MAN MAY BE CALLED A PILGRIM

WHO LEAVETH THE PLACE OF HIS BIRTH

After the diagnosis,

I went to the first church I could find.
I don't know any prayers,

I only know songs that have god broken down into them.

The woman to my left spoke Spanish.
Everything she knew

was in Spanish and even what she didn't
was in it, even death was in Spanish.

She looked up

from her language. I looked
up from my language, so this is what is

meant by prayer.

IN THE SHRINE OF THE HOLY DIRT

I said to the man,

My favorite word is *humility.*
He said his favorite word was *humility.*

Though we were already taller than a kneel.

Most people will tell you
their favorite word is *serendipity.*

Few, in fact, choose the dirt.

But when a man bends
it's his height
made wide before you.

REVIVAL

Some people say the Lord's Prayer.

I say, *I wanna die*
     I wanna die
     I wanna die

It's not what you think. It's happiness I'm after,
but it must include the root.

Don't we rise, in fact, downward?

The only trouble is
The only trouble is
The only trouble

is swallowing it back. So hard
for death to resume

its life in the body.

PALMISTRY

The hand used to have to be gloved,
used to have
to be kissed, a surrogate lip.

What is naked
drifts about the body

as heaven was
placed on certain peaks,
then the sky.

Your fingertip on my palm,
o point me
where god lives.

CIRCUITRY

Our messages go through zeroes and ones,
go broke, stripping down to figures. A riverbank,

and someone comes and takes
the clothes away,
and then the shore away, and you

wonder if love is not
simply the wish to go

on talking.

For "tired" read "attired."
For "agone" read "ago."

For the "ancients" are "hoary-headed,"
and the "finer," the "refiner."

Let the "food" be "meat"
and the "amazed" be "dismayed."

For we have struck "the unicorns,"
for they were fabulous.

Let "let" mean "not let"
and "prevent" mean "allow,"

so completely have these words
laid down with their shadows.

For "woman" is wife
and "belly" the body.

For he who "went hard" is now he who "drew near."
For "his summer parlour" is "our cool upper room."

And the "stranger" is changed,
for there is no farther than a "foreigner"

to come, except angels
and lovers whose comings alone

are comprehended
not their tongues.

THE PRIMER

She said, *I love you.*

He said nothing.

As if there were just one
of each word and the one
who used it, used it up.

In the history of language
the first obscenity was silence.

BIRDS OF EVERY WING SHALL DWELL WITHIN

variation on a poem by Marina Tsvetaeva

For once the god
paused pleased,
the maker of the plenty
of angels saw

how some rose engulfed
by their own wings,
while others fell to flapping
their nothing feathers.

He did not put
the differences on them,
is not the reason

I cry. I weep

because more even than
god, I worship
the messengers.

HOMESICKNESS

variation on a poem by Marina Tsvetaeva

Raw, ingrown, unrest.
Indifferent to me
now, the location
of my wholly aloneness,

stones that stumble me
home, a housing
as mine as anyone's
ward or fortress.

Indifferent to me also, veldtless
lion, the faces
that mow me down,
the human clique that casts me

out into
me, my lonely motive,
a polar bear
minus the ice.

Where I am unfit (and I refuse
to assume their sizes),
where I am lower than anyone,
the rung of my humanhood

is indifferent to me,
as are the enticements
of my native tongue,
its lactose lure. What does it matter

in what language I am
mistaken by anyone (unmeetable
readers, mouthers of headlines,
rumor-mongers)? They are at home

in this century,
whereas I am prior
to time, a log in the axed
avenue of trees.

My country so unmothered me
the keenest spy
could eye me over
and find no native taint.

Houses maroon me, temples empty.
They're all the same.
But if a single berry still cleaves
to that homeliest,

that rowantree . . . .

HOW TO PLAY HOUSE

To prepare for the visitor, you must move

the objects off
and shove the shoes
beneath the bed.

Where there is a hollow, put the paper.
Where there is a mother, put a father.

Put a third chair at the table,
empty but saved.

Where there was never a question,
seat a child. Where there is
no one to love,

put instructions.

THE RAVEN'S BOOK

Where presence is denied them
They fling their speech.
                    —Emily Dickinson

I

Are you still there? I didn't know

there could be this much room. Such a short word, *No*,
but how long they've been saying it.

They say men tend to head in the direction
of their handedness. So I look for you

on the right. It's not much to go on.
But of little, at least, there will never be shortage.

I want to tell you all the little wrongs between us,
the ones they don't arrest.

If you were here, you'd bend into me,
low as a fountain's stump of water, and whisper

Once everyone's dreamed, we will sleep.

11

Do you think there is such a thing as a happy memory?
Aren't the mountains in debt

to the valleys? Sometimes I think only sad memories
could truly be happy. They are final in the mind.

Consider the ravens, sayeth the lord,
for they neither sow nor reap, they keep nothing in store.

For which god feeds them.

III

Would you say you are getting closer?

In China, they say a three-legged raven lives inside the sun:
dawn, *dusk*, and *noon* are the names.

Whereas a man's legs are two and take sides.

I begin to lose track of you. If you are alive
you are looking at the moon

and I can trace the isosceles of our seeing.

IV

At first, I searched for your face.

Then, after many months, your clothing.
Then, the sudden absence

of spider webs and the shining of the dirt,
which are the signs of a human being.

Then I waited and continued to wait and made a mess

of your things
to be among them.

Then spring came, and no bird
resumed its egg.

v

Do you think there is such a thing as forgetting?

Sometimes I think it is the nearest
a thing can come
and not need a name.

Doesn't a house remain around us, a real house
for which only
the visible sign is lacking?

Beside it, the termites continue the tree.
The ravens continue the rabbit, ravenously.

Above it, sky
is like a blackboard

written on with erasers.

III

THE HUMANITIES

Tomorrow the man comes
to school me in the Fire.

You can lead a whole life surrounded by firemakers
and the putters out of fire
and think you have built a fire, and not have.

If the taming of blazes was the making of man,
I will have been a beast
until that hour when the man and I kneel down
with the tinder.

Also, no one has taught me how to die.

It is not listed
among the disciplines.

TWO THEORIES OF WESTERN ART

The docent says

in almost every masterpiece of classical art
the gods look like the people who worshipped them.

Whereas I know a man
who saves the anonymous faces
sold with the frames

and props them against the wall (and, in his wallet,
folds them with his family) till the day

when each is recognized.

UNDERSTUDIES

In Shakespeare, Love enters
through the eye
and Death, the ear.

Because the ear cannot close.
Because the ear is the organ of suffrage.

Because *death* is the foreignest word.

Because it is secret,
because we are

shared by this secret.

We met Judas during intermission
at his woodcarving shop.
Business was good, he said, but not as good
as the year he played Christ.
Some once, some never
get to be him. Me, I'd choose the role
of a shepherd in the outfield
or a starstruck sheep,
and I'd stage the birth instead
of the death: this time,
a musical. And not Christ's birth,
just any old child's.

So what, if it took ten years to make
a bass of the boy in the field,
so what, if the mothers must agree
to raise their girls as voices?

DRAMATIS PERSONAE

What is it you do, again?

What do you call a character
who is only put here
to foster an impenetrable plot?

A foil?

A human.

THIRD PERSON

Whatever you do, do not make me say *him*.

Him was not a word
in his presence.

To speak of what was is to hold it above its home,

a fish dripping
against a gunwale

Whereas inside the sea,
the fishes
do not drip.

THE GREAT FIRE

I can still hear our father calling us back,
sounding the All-Clear

as we stood at the edge of the lawn
panting off-stage of the flames.

We rehearsed disaster: out, out, or (if
a storm) in, in, all the poses like prayers

in different religions.

And I can hear him tell how Man first found it,
perched on a branch after lightning

and kept it from spreading,
everything is loved

till it spreads, that's what *weed* means:
plenty. And how he cured the rooms of dark,

which was their wont.

WEST HOUSE

I woke to him hunched
over the bed's edge,
red hair like fall breaking out in the thicket
and a beard about to come.

Him shaking his head, like I was the patient he was
in the helpless know of.

Or like a parent who could give
his child almost anything again, but birth.

Only when he was gone
did I fear him,
though he'd only done what I wished

the living would: return.

PRETERNATURAL

We happened on a tombstone
leaning against a tree.

No name had been engraved on it.

Only red needles had fallen and formed
a nest around
the indents for Christ.

I said, *I guess the person began to, but didn't die.*

You said, *Maybe its meanings are young yet*
and reached for my hand.

Then we saw
that a name had started
on the stone.

What is the name of our death.
Is it really stroke or rope, really fever or falling?

I would like to say,
My grandmother died of Lillian.
My grandfather of Anthony.
Anita of herself, and Nell of herself.
Of Daisy, did my dog die. And of blades, the grass.

We go forth in the name we lived.

I will die of Christina.
I was so called.

BLUEGRASS

Many people have wills. I have no will.
My entire family is buried in the dirt just shy of the Ohio
and west of a Krogers. I do not know
if my parents have reserved a similar plot.

People tend to be buried where they lived or scattered
where they wanted to be,
this is altogether strange to me.

I ought to be buried where I never lived,
because to be buried means
to never-live, or be scattered in a field far from want
because I've wanted already.

My grandmother said precious little but merely breathed in and in
as if the back of her were open and we were no longer in
the presence of the front. *Is it over?*
someone asked, of the inverted journeywork.

I put my hand to her mouth, from which a heat streamed
as if the alphabet were burning: some final fever
of the Bible and the merest mention made, of the contradictions
and the flickering signs, of how-to's and hearsays
and who she might have been if No had never been said to her

appeared before us without
hindrance, her face smoothed and blued,
so this was what Yes looked like.

ECHOES TUNED TO AN ORIGIN

You could say

we started branded, that what selves we were
grew around the sound,

a fleshly echo: we learned to follow who could say us.

Our names ushering us
further off.

Could say we began specified, singular, taut,
to each his own
mother, his own mattering.

How imperceptibly
time likened us, gently as a feather
abandons the bird.

The hair, the skin: it goes by so briefly the body,

answering now
to *You, there,* to *Stranger.*

NOTES

Forth A Raven: In the Book of Genesis, Noah sends forth a raven and a dove to test the status of the Flood. The dove returns, but the fate of the raven remains ambiguous.

Any Man May Be Called a Pilgrim Who Leaveth the Place of His Birth: The title is taken from Dante Gabriel Rossetti's ornate translation of Dante Alighieri's *Vita Nuova*.

Revival: "Don't we rise in fact downward?" is a question raised in César Vallejo's *Trilce* (translated by Clayton Eshleman).

In the Shrine of the Holy Dirt: A shrine in Chimayo, New Mexico, an earthen corridor of which is strewn with the crutches and wheelchairs of those who have purportedly been healed.

Circuitry: Echoes a line in Virginia Woolf's *The Voyage Out*.

Jubilat: In 1885, the American Old Testament Revision Company put forth a new edition of the Bible. The glossary included a brief but contentious list of the ways "in which it differs from the British Company."

The Raven's Book: "I am fairly in the raven's book" was once a way of saying "I am dying." The sequence was written in honor of Nadezhda Mandelstam's final letter to her husband, the poet Osip Mandelstam, which he never received. "No bird resumes its egg" was embedded in the letters of Emily Dickinson. For the notion of an invisible home that stretches over vast distances, I am indebted to Rilke.

Two Varieties of Passion Plays: The passion play has been performed by the villagers of Oberammergau, Germany, every ten years since the early 1600s when it was perceived to have warded off the Plague.

The Great Fire: Dedicated to my father—fireman, inventor, preserver.

RECENT TITLES FROM ALICE JAMES BOOKS

The Pitch, Tom Thompson
Landscapes I & II, Lesle Lewis
Here, Bullet, Brian Turner
The Far Mosque, Kazim Ali
Gloryland, Anne Marie Macari
Polar, Dobby Gibson
Pennyweight Windows: New & Selected Poems, Donald Revell
Matadora, Sarah Gambito
In the Ghost-House Acquainted, Kevin Goodan
The Devotion Field, Claudia Keelan
Into Perfect Spheres Such Holes Are Pierced, Catherine Barnett
Goest, Cole Swensen
Night of a Thousand Blossoms, Frank X. Gaspar
Mister Goodbye Easter Island, Jon Woodward
The Devil's Garden, Adrian Matejka
The Wind, Master Cherry, the Wind, Larissa Szporluk
North True South Bright, Dan Beachy-Quick
My Mojave, Donald Revell
Granted, Mary Szybist
Sails the Wind Left Behind, Alessandra Lynch
Sea Gate, Jocelyn Emerson
An Ordinary Day, Xue Di
The Captain Lands in Paradise, Sarah Manguso
Ladder Music, Ellen Doré Watson
Self and Simulacra, Liz Waldner
Live Feed, Tom Thompson
The Chime, Cort Day
Utopic, Claudia Keelan
Pity the Bathtub Its Forced Embrace of the Human Form, Matthea Harvey
Isthmus, Alice Jones
The Arrival of the Future, B.H. Fairchild
The Kingdom of the Subjunctive, Suzanne Wise
Camera Lyrica, Amy Newman
How I Got Lost So Close to Home, Amy Dryansky
The Art of the Lathe, B.H. Fairchild

ALICE JAMES BOOKS has been publishing exclusively poetry since 1973. One of the few presses in the country that is run collectively, the cooperative selects manuscripts for publication through both regional and national annual competitions. New regional authors become active members of the cooperative, participating in the editorial decisions of the press. The press, which historically has placed an emphasis on publishing women poets, was named for Alice James, sister of William and Henry, whose fine journal and gift for writing went unrecognized within her lifetime.

Typeset and Designed by Mike Burton

Printed by Thomson-Shore